AFRICAN-AMERICAN WRITERS AND JOURNALISTS

MARY HERTZ SCARBROUGH

TITLES IN THIS SERIES

AFRICAN-AMERICAN WRITERS AND JOURNALISTS

MARY HERTZ SCARBROUGH

MASON CREST
PHILADELPHIA

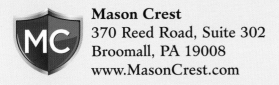

Mason Crest
370 Reed Road, Suite 302
Broomall, PA 19008
www.MasonCrest.com

Printed and bound in the United States of America.

CPSIA Compliance Information: Batch #MBC2012-6. For further information, contact Mason Crest at 1-866-MCP-Book.

First printing
1 3 5 7 9 8 6 4 2

Library of Congress Cataloging-in-Publication Data

Scarbrough, Mary Hertz.
  African American writers and journalists / Mary Hertz Scarbrough.
      p. cm. — (Major Black contributions from emancipation to civil rights)
  Includes bibliographical references and index.
  ISBN 978-1-4222-2376-5 (hc)
  ISBN 978-1-4222-2389-5 (pb)
  1. African American authors—Biography—Juvenile literature. 2. African American
  journalists—Biography—Juvenile literature. 3. African Americans—Intellectual
  life—Juvenile literature. I. Title.
  PS153.N5S33 2012
  810.9'896073—dc23
                                          2011051951

Publisher's note: All quotations in this book are taken from original sources, and contain the spelling and grammatical inconsistencies of the original texts.

Picture credits: courtesy Berea College: 37; courtesy The Heinz Awards: 55; Library of Congress: 8, 11, 13, 16, 19, 20, 23 (left), 24, 26, 30, 32, 36, 38, 39, 40, 42, 43, 45, 47; courtesy of the National Portrait Gallery, Smithsonian Institution, Washington, D.C.: 35; Ohio Historical Society: 21, 23 (right); © 2012 Photos.com, a division of Getty Images: 7; courtesy Random House: 44; Olga Besnard / Shutterstock.com: 54; Robert Pernell / Shutterstock.com: 52; Third World Press (http://www.twpbooks.com): 50; United Nations Photo: 48; Wikimedia Commons: 3.

TABLE OF CONTENTS

INTRODUCTION

Dr. Marc Lamont Hill

I t is impossible to tell the story of America without telling the story of Black Americans. From the struggle to end slavery, all the way to the election of the first Black president, the Black experience has been a window into America's own movement toward becoming a "more perfect union." Through the tragedies and triumphs of Blacks in America, we gain a more full understanding of our collective history and a richer appreciation of our collective journey. This book series, MAJOR BLACK CONTRIBUTIONS FROM EMANCIPATION TO CIVIL RIGHTS, spotlights that journey by showing the many ways that Black Americans have been a central part of our nation's development.

In this series, we are reminded that Blacks were not merely objects of history, swept up in the winds of social and political inevitability. Rather, since the end of legal slavery, Black men and women have actively fought for their own rights and freedoms. It is through their courageous efforts (along with the efforts of allies of all races) that Blacks are able to enjoy ever increasing levels of inclusion in American democracy. Through this series, we learn the names and stories of some of the most important contributors to our democracy.

But this series goes far beyond the story of slavery to freedom. The books in this series also demonstrate the various contributions of Black Americans to the nation's social, cultural, technological, and intellectual growth. While these books provide new and deeper insights into the lives and stories of familiar figures like Martin Luther King, Michael Jordan, and Oprah Winfrey, they also introduce readers to the contributions of countless heroes who have often been pushed to the margins of history. In reading this series, we are able to see that Blacks have been key contributors across every field of human endeavor.

   Although this is a series about Black Americans, it is important and necessary reading for everyone. While readers of color will find enormous purpose and pride in uncovering the history of their ancestors, these books should also create similar sentiments among readers of all races and ethnicities. By understanding the rich and deep history of Blacks, a group often ignored or marginalized in history, we are reminded that everyone has a story. Everyone has a contribution. Everyone matters.

   The insights of these books are necessary for creating deeper, richer, and more inclusive classrooms. More importantly, they remind us of the power and possibility of individuals of all races, places, and traditions. Such insights not only allow us to understand the past, but to create a more beautiful future.

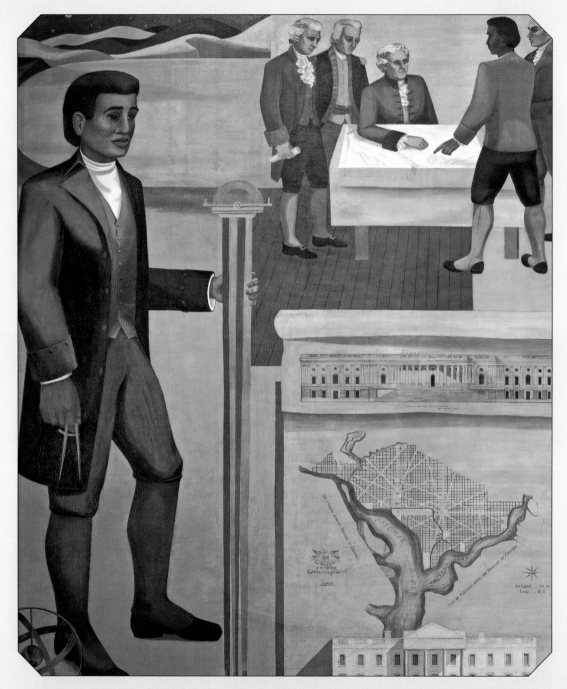

This mural depicts the Revolutionary War-era surveyor, inventor, and astronomer Benjamin Banneker, who wrote and published a successful almanac during the 1790s.

1

EARLY AFRICAN-AMERICAN WRITERS

In 1619, ships with Africans on board began to land in the British colonies in North America. These Africans did not ask to come to America. They were forced to come. Once here, they were forced to work. These first Africans might have been slaves. It's also possible they were servants who would gain their freedom after working for a certain number of years. Soon, however, slavery was a part of life in America. The system of slavery lasted nearly 250 years, until after the American Civil War (1861–1865).

African-American slaves often weren't allowed to read or write. Although there were some free blacks in America, they generally had few opportunities to attend school, either. For that reason, some of the first African American "writers" could neither read nor write. Those who couldn't write told others who could what to write. Some, but not all, of the earliest black American writers were slaves.

In 1746, a female slave named Lucy Terry made up a poem. This is the first known poem by an African American. It was about an Indian attack near Terry's home. Two families were killed. For many years people passed along the poem by singing it and repeating it. Lucy's poem wasn't written down and published until more than 100 years after her death.

THE FIRST PUBLISHED WORDS

The first published writing by African Americans appeared about 15 years after Lucy Terry composed her poem. Briton Hammon, a black slave from Massachusetts, wrote about his adventures. He was on a ship that sank off the coast of Florida. Hammon escaped in a small boat, but was then captured by Native Americans. They sold him to a Spanish captain, who took Hammon to the Spanish settlement at St. Augustine, Florida. While there he was held in a dungeon and forced to work as a slave. Hammon eventually gained his freedom. He traveled to London, then back to New England, where he was reunited with his former master. Hammon's story was published in Boston in 1760.

The first published poem by a black writer came about the same time Briton Hammon's tale appeared. The author, Jupiter Hammon, had been a slave his entire life. Unlike most slaves, he was allowed to go to school. One of his poems was published in 1761. He later published other poems and essays. In 1786, when Jupiter was about 70 years old, he gave a famous speech. It was titled "An Address to the Negroes of the State of New York." Jupiter said he did "not wish to be free." However, he said he would be "glad if others, especially the young negroes, were free." He said that slaves should obey their masters, but that they should also try to get an education. Jupiter also encouraged white slave-owners to consider freeing their black slaves. The speech was published in 1787.

One of Jupiter Hammon's poems, published in 1778, was addressed to Phillis Wheatley. She

— Did You Know? —

Despite having the same last name, Briton Hammon and Jupiter Hammon were not related. The name Hammon was probably derived from the Biblical figure Ham, a son of Noah. In the Bible, Noah says that Ham and his descendants would be slaves. Ham's descendants were thought to be black Africans. For hundreds of years, Christians used Bible verses about Ham to justify the enslavement of blacks.

was a young African-American woman who had become a famous poet. Wheatley is the first African-American woman to have a book of poetry published.

Phillis was named for the ship that brought her from West Africa in 1761, when she was about eight years old. A Boston merchant named John Wheatley bought her as a servant for his wife, Susanna. The Wheatleys taught Phillis how to read and write. Her first poems were published in a newspaper in 1767. Her poetry soon made Phillis Wheatley famous in both Great Britain and in the American colonies. Although many people liked her poems, no American printer would publish them in a book. Wheatley had to go to London to have her book of poems published in 1773. Her poems were mostly about her Christian faith.

This portrait of Phillis Wheatley appeared at the front of her book *Poems on Various Subjects, Religious and Moral*, which was published in London in 1773.

Despite her fame, Wheatley died poor and alone in 1784. However, Phillis Wheatley's poetry is still studied today. Modern African-American writers like Alice Walker have called her an inspiration.

THE FIRST SCIENCE WRITER

The first black science writer was Benjamin Banneker. He was born to a family of free black farmers in Maryland in 1731. Banneker attended school until he was old enough to work on the farm. While working as a farmer, he found ways to teach himself. When Banneker was 22, he constructed one of the first clocks built in America. He also learned a lot about astronomy and math.

Between 1792 and 1797, Banneker put his knowledge of these subjects to use. Each year he published an almanac. Each had a calendar and

included sunrise and sunset times, proper planting times for farmers, the dates of religious festivals, and other information. His almanacs were very successful.

Banneker also worked as a surveyor. In 1791, he helped mark the boundaries of the city that would become Washington, D.C.

In 1793, Banneker wrote a famous letter to Thomas Jefferson. He argued that if the United States was to be a free nation, it was wrong not to grant freedom to African-American slaves.

HELPING BRING AN END TO SLAVERY

Frederick Douglass began his life as a slave. Born in Maryland in 1818, he learned to read and write as a youngster. During his teens, he worked on a farm. There he was whipped daily and nearly starved. Douglass later said he "was broken in body, soul, and spirit." Douglass tried several times to escape. He finally succeeded in 1838.

Slave Narratives

Slave narratives were popular in the years leading up to the Civil War. They helped convince people that slavery was wrong. Much like an action movie captures an audience's attention today, slave narratives fascinated 19th century readers. They described beatings for misbehavior or attempted escapes. They told how families could be split up and sent to different places. They revealed the often back-breaking work that slaves were forced to endure.

Slave narratives could also show glimpses of bright spots. They told about the family life, friendship, music, and religious beliefs of slaves.

Some former slaves took their stories on the road. They were often popular speakers in the Northern states and in Europe. Two famous narratives are by Harriet Jacobs and Sojourner Truth.

Douglass worked hard to educate himself once he escaped. He met William Lloyd Garrison, a white newspaper writer and publisher. Garrison was an abolitionist, someone who worked to free slaves. He was impressed by Douglass's story. He hired Douglass to tell others about his life as a slave. Douglass was a brilliant speaker. He became famous.

In 1845, Douglass wrote his autobiography. It was a bestseller. Soon he started the *North Star* newspaper. His newspaper supported abolition and other causes,

Frederick Douglass

Frederick Douglass's *North Star* newspaper was named for the brightest star visible in North America. Runaway slaves would use the north star as their guide when escaping to the northern U.S. states or Canada, where they could be free.

such as women's rights. He ran a newspaper or a magazine for many years. He also wrote three books about his life. Frederick Douglass once wrote, "I discovered that the power of the word is the best means to bring about permanent positive changes, both for myself and others."

Unlike Douglass, William Cooper Nell had never been a slave. He had been born to a free black family in Massachusetts. However, Nell also wrote about the injustice of slavery and racial prejudice. His articles appeared in both *The North Star* and in Garrison's newspaper, *The Liberator*.

Nell was the first African American to write about the history of blacks in the United States. He wrote books about African-American patriots who had served during the Revolutionary War and the War of 1812. Without his work, these stories would probably have been lost forever.

While Nell and Douglass used newspaper writing to promote abolition, James Monroe Whitfield used poetry. A barber by trade, Whitfield wrote poems condemning slavery. The opening lines from Whitfield's poem "America" (1853) contrast what Americans believe their country stands for and what it actually is:

America, it is to thee,
    Thou boasted land of liberty, —
It is to thee I raise my song
    Thou land of blood, and crime, and wrong.
It is to thee, my native land,
    From whence has issued many a band
To tear the black man from his soil,
    And force him here to delve and toil;
Chained on your blood-bemoistened sod,
    Cringing beneath a tyrant's rod,
Stripped of those rights which Nature's God
    Bequeathed to all the human race,
Bound to a petty tyrant's nod,
    Because he wears a paler face.

THE FIRST AFRICAN AMERICAN FICTION

Almost all African-American writing before the Civil War was nonfiction. Harriet Wilson wrote fiction. Wilson was a free woman from New Hampshire. She wrote the first novel by an African-American woman.

Wilson's 1859 book *Our Nig* was inspired by her own life. The book was unusual because it was set in the North. Also, its main character, Frado, was not a slave. She was a servant for a white family and was free to leave when she turned 18. The book is about the discrimination and abuse she faced while free. Another major character was a black man who pretended to be an escaped slave.

== Did You Know? ==

African-American writer Victor Séjour (1817–1874) moved from New Orleans to Paris, where his first fiction story was published in 1837. The story, titled "Le Mulâtre," is about a slave who murders his master. It wasn't translated from French into English for more than 100 years.

He made his living touring and lecturing about his so-called life of slavery. Wilson's novel pointed out that even without slavery, mistreatment of African Americans was common, even in the North.

In his writings, including his bestselling autobiography *Up From Slavery*, Booker T. Washington explained his belief that African Americans needed education and vocational training so they could succeed economically in post–Civil War America.

2

FICTION AND NONFICTION AFTER THE CIVIL WAR

The end of the Civil War was not the end of racial inequality. In some ways, the lives of African Americans changed little. Black writers and journalists of the time worked to help improve things. People often had different opinions how best to do this.

Two of the best-known African-American writers in the years after the war were Booker T. Washington and W.E.B. Du Bois. As the years went by, their writings and speeches reflected their different views. The differences in their approaches to achieving equality for African Americans are still being discussed in the 21st century.

THE MOST POWERFUL AFRICAN AMERICAN OF HIS DAY

Booker T. Washington (1856–1915) has been called the most powerful African American of his day. Washington was born a slave. He was forbidden to learn to read and white. Yet as an adult he gave advice to several presidents.

Washington wrote three autobiographies. *Up From Slavery* told about his early life. He did not know who his father was. After the Civil War, he worked in a salt mine. He finally made it to school. He became a teacher. That led to a job in charge of a new school in Tuskegee, Alabama.

Fame came after he gave a speech in Atlanta, Georgia, in 1895. In it, Washington said that providing equal rights for African Americans would benefit all Americans, no matter their color. He said that educational training and hard work was the best way for blacks to achieve equality. Force should not be used to bring about change, Washington said. And although he wanted equality for black Americans, Washington felt it was acceptable for blacks and whites to be socially segregated. He said that blacks and whites could work together like fingers on a hand. Even though fingers work together, they stay separate.

The majority of Americans, including many blacks, agreed with Washington's speech at the time. Eventually, though, some blacks began to criticize this approach. They thought African Americans were not making progress fast enough. They argued that black Americans needed to demand their rights.

Tuskegee Institute

This school was founded on July 4, 1881, in Tuskegee, Alabama. It was created to train teachers, workers in industry, farming, and similar jobs. Booker T. Washington was its first leader. He was just 25 years old. He built the school from the ground up. He headed the college until he died in 1915.

Washington was an excellent organizer. He was very good at raising money. Students built their own buildings and produced their own food for the school. The first classes took place in a one-room building. There were 30 students. By the time Washington died, Tuskegee had grown to about 1,500. Today there are about 3,000 students. It is called Tuskegee University.

Famous graduates include the writer Ralph Ellison and musician Lionel Richie. George Washington Carver taught and researched there for nearly 50 years. He is known for his work with peanuts and sweet potatoes. His work helped improve the lives of Southern farmers.

AN ALTERNATIVE APPROACH

W.E.B. Du Bois (1868–1963) was one of those who thought Washington was wrong. Du Bois grew up in a mostly white community in Massachusetts. When he was 15, he got a job in his hometown writing for the *New York Globe*.

When he attended college in Tennessee, Du Bois experienced severe discrimination for the first time. Washington wanted slow change. Du Bois demanded it right away. Washington pushed for schools where blacks could learn practical job training. Du Bois wanted a more typical college education. He said legal rights and integration should come ahead of education.

Du Bois himself was highly educated. In 1895 he became the first African American to earn a Ph.D. from Harvard University. His long life involved research, teaching, civil rights work, and more. He wrote many books, speeches, and articles. He helped start the National Association for the Advancement of Colored People (NAACP) in 1909. He edited magazines, including *The Crisis*, the NAACP magazine. One of

W.E.B. Du Bois was a major scholar and civil rights activist of the early 20th century. His writings influenced many people.

his best-known books was *The Souls of Black Folk* (1903), which criticized Washington's approach.

Washington's personal beliefs were more complicated than Du Bois and other critics realized. Publicly, he wrote and spoke in favor of slow change. This meant many white Americans agreed with him. His white supporters sent money to help Tuskegee Institute. Secretly, however, Washington worked in other ways to further the advancement of equality. He quietly

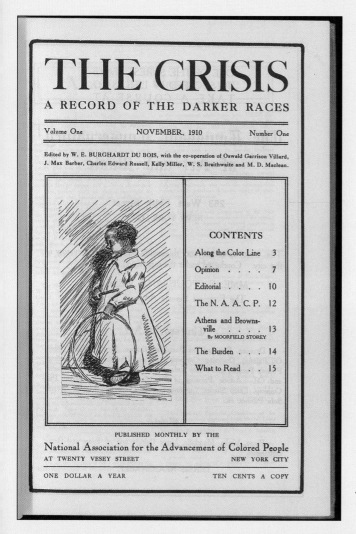

The first issue of *The Crisis*, the journal of the National Association for the Advancement of Colored People, which was edited by W.E.B. Du Bois. *The Crisis* not only reported on NAACP activities, it also provided a forum for talented African-American writers to publish their poems, short stories, and editorial commentary.

used some of the money he received from white supporters to help some black newspapers. He also secretly paid for lawyers to file court cases against discriminatory Jim Crow laws that prevented blacks from voting, serving on juries, or riding in train cars with whites.

This double life meant Washington had many black critics. On the other hand, by working in secret, he was able to accomplish great things at Tuskegee. If he had been open about his civil rights activities, he would have lost his support among whites.

PIONEERING JOURNALIST

Years before Du Bois and Washington were arguing about the best approach for equality, one African-American woman had already become

famous. She did so by working for it in a number of ways. Frances Ellen Watkins Harper (1825–1911) had a long writing career before and after the Civil War. She wrote plays, novels, essays, and poetry. People loved to hear her speak.

After the Civil War she traveled throughout the South. Although slavery was gone, she saw that many of the newly freed African Americans still lived in horrendous conditions. Equality for the races was her main goal, but she was also in favor of allowing women the right to vote. She also spoke and wrote about the evils of alcohol.

In *Sketches of Southern Life* (1872) Harper told stories of slavery and reconstruction. The book was written just as African Americans talked. This was a new way of writing for a black writer.

In 1892, Harper published her only novel, *Iola Leroy*. The book begins on a Mississippi plantation just as the Civil War is ending. The main character, Iola, has grown up not knowing that her light-skinned mother is black. When her father dies, she learns the truth. Iola and her mother are treated poorly. Iola and her mother move to the North but still face prejudice. Like her mother, Iola could pass as a white person. She has to choose whether or not to do so. Iola loses a job when her employer realizes she is black. In the end,

One of Frances Harper's most popular poems was "Bury Me in a Free Land," which was written in the late 1850s. The narrator of the poem claims she will be unable to rest after death if the unjust slave system continues to exist. The poem concludes with these lines:

> I ask no monument, proud and high
>   To arrest the gaze of the passers-by
> All that my yearning spirit craves
>   Is bury me not in a land of slaves.

This photo of Harper was taken in the 1890s.

> ### — Did You Know? —
>
> Some people thought Frances E.W. Harper had to be a fake. They thought she was too good at what she did. Some people thought she was a white woman pretending to be black. Others thought she might be a man.

Iola decides to live as a black person. She moves back to the South. Iola and other characters spend their lives helping improve the lives of other African Americans.

Iola Leroy was very popular. Using fiction was a way for Harper to talk about issues she cared deeply about. She even used parts of her own speeches in the book.

Harper's accomplishments as a writer were mostly forgotten after she died in 1911. Eventually, though, people began to recognize how much she had accomplished. She was a popular, successful writer during a time when African Americans and women both struggled far more than white men.

POPULAR POET

Frances Harper was well known for her poetry. During her lifetime Paul Laurence Dunbar (1872–1906) became even more famous for his. Dunbar's parents were both former slaves. His mother loved poetry, songs, and storytelling. She passed this love to her son. At six years old he began to write poetry. As the only black student at his high school, he edited the school paper. He was also president of the literary society.

Dunbar wanted to go to college but could not afford it. He ran a hotel elevator and wrote in his spare time. He studied

> ### — Did You Know? —
>
> Paul Dunbar and Orville Wright were high school classmates and friends in Dayton, Ohio. In 1890, Orville Wright and his brother Wilbur ran a small printing business. They printed a newspaper edited by Dunbar for the black community, the *Dayton Tattler*. The Wright brothers would go on to build the first successful airplane in 1903.

At the end of the 19th century, Paul Laurence Dunbar was the most famous black writer in the United States. Although his reputation was made on his poetry, Dunbar also was a skilled short story writer, novelist, and playwright. He wrote songs—including one for the Tuskegee Institute. After his death, some of Dunbar's poems were set to music; sheet music for one such tune is pictured at the left.

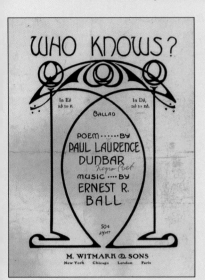

English and American poets as he figured out his own style. In the end, Dunbar wrote in both standard English and in African-American dialect. The poems written the way blacks talked reflect the singing and storytelling from his childhood. He called this poetry "jingle in a broken tongue." Although those poems made him famous, Dunbar was bothered that sometimes his more formal poems seemed to be overlooked.

Dunbar died young but his writing influenced writers who came after him. In particular, African-American poets of the 1920s praised and imitated him.

Dunbar also wrote four novels. *The Sport of the Gods* tells the story of a family whose father is wrongly accused of a crime. He goes to jail instead of a white man. This book influenced the writing of African-American novelist Richard Wright 50 years later.

CONSIDER THE FACTS.

During six weeks of the months of March and April just past, twelve colored men were lynched in Georgia, the reign of outlawry culminating in the torture and hanging of the colored preacher, Elijah Strickland, and the burning alive of Samuel Wilkes, alias Hose, Sunday, April 23, 1899.

The real purpose of these savage demonstrations is to teach the Negro that in the South he has no rights that the law will enforce. Samuel Hose was burned to teach the Negroes that no matter what a white man does to them, they must not resist. Hose, a servant, had killed Cranford, his employer. An example must be made. Ordinary punishment was deemed inadequate. This Negro must be burned alive. To make the burning a certainty the charge of outrage was invented, and added to the charge of murder. The daily press offered reward for the capture of Hose and then openly incited the people to burn him as soon as caught. The mob carried out the plan in every savage detail.

Of the twelve men lynched during that reign of unspeakable barbarism, only one was even charged with an assault upon a woman. Yet Southern apologists justify their savagery on the ground that Negroes are lynched only because of their crimes against women.

The Southern press champions burning men alive, and says, "Consider the facts." The colored people join issue and also say, "Consider the facts." The colored people of Chicago employed a detective to go to Georgia, and his report in this pamphlet gives the facts. We give here the details of the lynching as they were reported in the Southern papers, then follows the report of the true facts as to the cause of the lynchings, as learned by the investigation. We submit all to the sober judgment of the Nation, confident that, in this cause, as well as all others, "Truth is mighty and will prevail."

IDA B. WELLS-BARNETT.

2939 Princeton Avenue, Chicago, June 20, 1899.

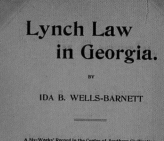

Lynch Law in Georgia.

BY

IDA B. WELLS-BARNETT

A Six-Weeks' Record in the Center of Southern Civilization, As Faithfully Chronicled by the "Atlanta Journal" and the "Atlanta Constitution."

ALSO THE FULL REPORT OF LOUIS P. LE VIN,

The Chicago Detective Sent to Investigate the Burning of Samuel Hose, the Torture and Hanging of Elijah Strickland, the Colored Preacher, and the Lynching of Nine Men for Alleged Arson.

This Pamphlet is Circulated by Chicago Colored Citizens. 2939 Princeton Avenue, Chicago.

1899

The cover (right) and first page of the 1899 pamphlet *Lynch Law in Georgia*, written by journalist and activist Ida B. Wells-Barnett. Between 1880 and 1900, mob violence in Georgia aimed at African Americans grew steadily. The violence peaked in 1899 when 27 lynchings occurred. Among the most savage was the April 23, 1899, lynching of Sam Hose, a black farmer accused of killing his white employer. A mob removed Hose from jail, tortured him, and burned him at the stake. His charred knuckles were displayed in an Atlanta grocer's store window as a trophy. Ida B. Wells-Barnett and her friends hired Louis P. Le Vin, a white private detective, to investigate Hose's lynching and those of ten other black men.

3

JOURNALISTS IN THE LATE 19TH AND EARLY 20TH CENTURIES

The number of black newspapers exploded after the Civil War. About 500 started up between the end of the war and the start of the 20th century. They often had humble beginnings. Black churches often loaned their printing presses. Black newspapers sprang up everywhere, from Texas to California to Indiana to Nebraska. Many didn't stay in business very long.

Black newspapers provided information that people couldn't find in white newspapers. Newspapers were passed from hand to hand and shared with many others. They were often read aloud. They provided an African-American viewpoint.

If a black newspaper in the South printed something that whites didn't like, trouble could follow. Northern newspapers had more freedom to print what they wanted. Ida Wells learned first-hand about the danger of angering Southern whites.

FEARLESS CRUSADER

Ida B. Wells (1862–1931) was born in Mississippi. Her parents, both slaves, taught her how to read. She became a teacher in Memphis. An experience on a train ride put her on the path to journalism instead. Her train car was for whites only. Wells was asked to move to a different one.

In addition to her writing for African-American civil rights, Ida Wells-Barnett also supported equal rights for American women.

She refused. She sued the railroad and wrote about her experience.

For a while Wells kept her teaching job and worked as a journalist and editor. Then she lost her teaching job for writing about differences between white and black schools. She wrote for a newspaper called the *Evening Star*. In 1889 she became part owner of another Memphis newspaper, called the *Free Speech and Headlight*. This black newspaper published many articles on racial injustice.

Wells risked her life by writing about and speaking against horrible murders of African Americans called lynchings. Lynching was a punishment, usually death by hanging, carried out by angry mobs. There was no trial. Often, the only "crime" was that the person was black and outspoken. Lynchings were common. From 1882 to 1919, about 3,000 African Americans were lynched. This is an average of more than one a week.

In 1892, three of Wells's friends were lynched. They had owned a grocery store that some people claimed was taking business away from a white-owned store. Wells wrote an angry article telling African Americans to leave Memphis or to boycott white-owned businesses. "There is, therefore, only one thing left to do; save our money and leave a town which will neither protect our lives and property, nor give us a fair trial in the courts, but takes us out and murders us in cold blood when accused by white persons," she wrote. She said that lynching was a way for whites to get rid of black Americans who were successful or politically active.

Wells's words caused an uproar. Her office was destroyed. Fortunately, she was out of town at the time. She was warned that her life was in danger,

Segregation and "Jim Crow" Laws

During the late 1870s, many states and municipalities passed laws to segregate public places, such as schools, restaurants, theaters, hospitals, cemeteries, forms of transportation like trains and buses, and even drinking fountains. These laws became known as "Jim Crow laws." (*Jim Crow* was the name of a lazy and foolish African-American character in 19th century minstrel shows.) Jim Crow laws were common in the South, although there was also some segregation in the northern states. The Jim Crow laws created two societies existing uncomfortably together, one black and one white.

The Thirteenth, Fourteenth, and Fifteenth Amendments to the U.S. Constitution were supposed to give black Americans the same rights that white Americans had. However, over time the interpretation of those Constitutional amendments changed. In 1896, the U.S. Supreme Court issued an important decision in the case *Plessy v. Ferguson*. The Court ruled that blacks could legally be separated from whites, so long as the blacks had access to similar facilities or services as whites. In theory, the schools, hospitals, and other facilities for African Americans were said to be "separate but equal" to those for whites. In reality, whites almost always had the advantage. The *Plessy v. Ferguson* decision meant that the Jim Crow laws could remain in existence. Most were not repealed until the 1950s and 1960s.

Segregation put African Americans at a disadvantage. In addition to the unfair laws, African Americans were expected to behave in certain ways in the South. A black person could not shake hands with a white person, for example. A black person was expected to defer to a white person with respect, but blacks could not expect such respect in return. African Americans were expected to step off the sidewalk to make way for whites. They had to give white motorists the right-of-way at intersections. The list of expected behaviors was long. An African American who did not follow this unwritten code of behavior risked being attacked, and possibly lynched.

so she stayed away for 30 years. Chasing her out of Memphis did not stop Wells, though. She continued her writing about lynching. She gave many lectures, both in the United States and Great Britain. Her writing helped to inspire anti-lynching campaigns in both the North and the South.

Ida Wells continued writing even after she married Ferdinand L.

T. Thomas Fortune

Timothy Thomas Fortune (1856–1928) is hardly a household name today. But during the late 19th century he was the country's leading black journalist. Born a slave, after the civil war he earned an education. Then he began working for newspapers. By 1881, he had moved to New York City. He started out as a printer at a white newspaper. Within a few years he started his own newspaper. The paper, which came to be called *New York Age*, was the top black newspaper of its day.

Fortune's writing was very forceful. He called for action by African Americans. More than once he was arrested for his outspokenness. He paid a price for it. Businesses were not always willing to advertise in his paper. Eventually he received help from an unlikely source: Booker T. Washington. Although they seemed to have opposite approaches toward achieving equality for African Americans, the men became close friends. Fortune lent a hand with some of Washington's writing. Washington gave Fortune money to help support his newspaper. The Tuskegee Institute president also benefited from having Fortune's paper publicly defend his ideas.

When Ida B. Wells's Memphis newspaper office was destroyed, Fortune invited her to write for the *New York Age*. The newspaper published her stories about the horrors of lynching in the South. Fortune himself toured the South and wrote stories about racism and Jim Crow laws.

Fortune left the *New York Age* in 1907 because of a nervous breakdown. He continued writing and editing newspapers on and off for the rest of his life.

Barnett in 1895. She used her words and voice to campaign for women's rights. She helped start the NAACP and other organizations. She used her pen to attack injustice until the end of her life.

POWERFUL NEWSPAPERS

Another hugely influential newspaper person of the time was Robert Abbott (1870–1940). He started a paper called the *Chicago Defender* in 1905, in his landlord's kitchen. He printed 300 copies of his first edition, then took to the streets to sell it. Within five years the paper had started to attract a national audience.

Abbott made a very smart move. He got his paper into the South, where 90 percent of African Americans lived in 1910. In Chicago, Abbott could print things that no Southern black editor could get away with. It wasn't easy to get the *Defender* distributed, though. Abbott got train porters to smuggle the newspapers onto their trains. (Porters were usually black men.) The porters tossed bundles into the countryside. Later the papers could be picked up and handed out. By 1919, 130,000 copies of the *Chicago Defender* were being printed each week. Because the papers were passed from reader to reader, it's estimated that more than 400,000 people were reading each issue of the *Defender*.

Abbott's journalistic style at the *Defender* was similar to popular white newspapers of the time. In other words, he used yellow journalism. This meant that headlines weren't always backed up by facts. For instance, in January 1917, the *Defender* announced the Great Northern Migration. This was part of an ongoing campaign by Abbott. On May 15, 1917, blacks were supposed to leave the South, the newspaper said. It said trains headed north would be offering lower fares that day. Later the *Defender* came clean. There were no lower fares. In fact, no special arrangements of any sort had been made. By that time, though, thousands of blacks were getting ready to move. With the encouragement of black newspapers like the *Chicago Defender*, more than 400,000 African Americans migrated north between 1916 and 1918.

Another newspaper with a humble beginning was *The Pittsburgh*

To reach African-American readers, the largest black newspapers were distributed in many cities. In this photo from the 1940s, two people look at a display in the Chicago office of the *Pittsburgh Courier*, one of the major black newspapers of the early 20th century.

Courier. It started out small. Over time, it became as widely read as Abbott's paper. This was due in part to publisher Robert Lee Vann's development of as many as 14 different editions throughout the country, from Texas to New York.

Vann ran the paper from 1910 until his death in 1940. He encouraged readers to be active and work for change. In the 1932 presidential election, he wrote that black voters should stop voting for Abraham Lincoln's party. He said Republicans were failing African Americans. It was time to support Franklin D. Roosevelt and the Democrats. Many voters agreed with him.

THE BATTLES KEEP COMING

Out on the West Coast, an educated black woman named Charlotta Bass (1874–1969) had little newspaper experience. She had a job selling subscriptions to the *California Eagle* newspaper. When the paper's founder became sick, he asked Bass to work as editor. When the owner died in 1912, she took over the *California Eagle*. For almost 40 years, she used the *Eagle* to fight for equality for African Americans.

One of Bass's first battles was against the movie industry in California. In 1915 she tried to stop a racist movie, *The Birth of a Nation*, from being made. The movie portrayed African Americans as lazy, dishonest, and violent. Although her campaign did not succeed, people respected her effort.

Over the years, Bass often used her newspaper to argue against job discrimination. Many companies and government agencies refused to hire African Americans. Thanks to her editorials, in 1917 the Los Angeles fire department hired its first black fireman. In another case, during the early 1930s she convinced hundreds of readers to cancel their phone service. They told the phone company it was because they wouldn't hire blacks. Finally, the Southern California Telephone Company agreed to hire black workers.

Bass also fought against rules that kept blacks from buying houses in white neighborhoods, and against segregated schools. Her life was threatened time and again. She told her husband that if they were killed, it would be for a good cause.

Bass retired from the newspaper business in 1951. In 1952 she was the Progressive Party's candidate for vice president of the United States. When she was 70, she turned her garage into a place where voters could register. She wanted people of color to pull together to change things.

The Importance of Black Newspapers

Black newspapers in the late 19th and early 20th centuries gave their African-American readers a sense of community, pride, and purpose that they could not find in mainstream papers of the time. Newspaperman Vernon Jarrett (1918–2004), a founder of the National Association of Black Journalists, explained this feeling in the PBS documentary *The Black Press: Soldiers Without Swords*:

> We didn't exist in the other [white] papers. We were neither born, we didn't get married, we didn't die, we didn't fight in any wars, we never participated in anything of scientific achievement. We were truly invisible unless we committed a crime. And in the black press, the negro press, we did get married. They showed us our babies when born. They showed us graduating. The showed our Ph.Ds.

The poet, playwright, and activist Langston Hughes was a major figure of the Harlem Renaissance. He encouraged other African-American writers to take pride in being part of the black community and to write honestly about the lives and experiences of African Americans.

THE HARLEM RENAISSANCE

After World War I ended in November 1918, Americans were ready for some fun. Life had been hard during the war years. By the early 1920s the country was prospering. Many people still had money to spend after housing, food, and other needs were paid for. All in all, this was a boom time. In many cases, it wasn't only whites who were thriving. African Americans were too.

A "renaissance" is something new that is created, or a revival of something that has been forgotten. The Harlem Renaissance is the name for an African-American cultural movement that flourished after World War I. The Harlem Renaissance was centered in a New York City neighborhood called Harlem. By the 1920s, about 175,000 African Americans lived in Harlem.

One aspect of the Harlem Renaissance was that African Americans took greater pride in their heritage and accomplishments. Some blacks believed that they could "uplift the race" and challenge racism through literature, art, music, and other forms of expression. During the Harlem Renaissance, black writers tried to increase awareness about unjust treatment. W.E.B. Du Bois, who had already been writing for many years, was a huge influence. African-American writers also celebrated their unique culture. They encouraged a sense of unity among American blacks. As a result, white Americans took notice of black creative arts in a way that they never had before.

BELOVED POET

One of the writers Du Bois influenced was Langston Hughes (1902–1967). He has been called the most influential African-American poet of the Harlem Renaissance. During high school, Du Bois's book *The Souls of Black Folk* spoke to Hughes about racism. He was also influenced by white poets such as Walt Whitman and Carl Sandburg. Paul Laurence Dunbar's dialect poems shaped his writing too.

Hughes was barely out of high school when his poem "The Negro Speaks of Rivers" was published in Du Bois's magazine, *The Crisis*. The poem reflected Hughes's pride in his heritage. In a 1926 essay, Hughes wrote that young black writers "intend to express our individual dark-skinned selves without fear of shame."

Hughes continued writing long after the Harlem Renaissance ended in the early 1930s. Until his death in 1967, he wrote poetry, plays, fiction

"I, Too"

I, too, sing America
I am the darker brother.
They send me to eat in the kitchen
When company comes,
But I laugh,
And eat well,
And grow strong.

Tomorrow,
I'll be at the table
When company comes.
Nobody'll dare
Say to me,
"Eat in the kitchen,"
Then.

Besides,
They'll see how beautiful I am
And be ashamed—

I, too, am America.

—Langston Hughes

novels and short stories, nonfiction, books for children, and more. His work is prized for many reasons, such as for the way he captured the rhythm of African-American music and speech. Hughes's love of humanity shines throughout his work.

BRINGING ATTENTION TO BLACK WRITERS AND CULTURE

The writing of Langston Hughes and other black writers of the 1920s came to the attention of white Americans partly because of Alain Locke. Locke was a respected African-American scholar and educator. In 1925, he edited a book called *The New Negro: An Interpretation*. Locke included the best African-American fiction, poetry, plays, and essays. The book brought the work of outstanding black writers to the attention of white audiences. It also helped the writers see themselves as part of a bigger movement. Their skills could help African-Americans gain equality with whites and improve American society.

Locke encouraged poets like Countee Cullen (1903–1946) and Claude McKay (1889–1948). Cullen typically wrote very structured poems. He was among the most famous black poets of the time. McKay had grown up in Jamaica, but came to the United States in 1912. He was outspoken about tough racial issues, and liked to write about the working class.

Countee Cullen

Another African-American scholar, educator, and writer who helped focus attention on other black writers was James Weldon Johnson (1871–1938). Johnson had worked as a U.S. diplomat, serving in Venezuela and Nicaragua. His novel *The Autobiography of an Ex-Colored Man* (1912) helped bring attention to social problems that African-Americans faced. In 1922 Johnson edited *The Book of American Negro Poetry*. He also wrote two books on spirituals.

Educator, writer, and activist James Weldon Johnson (1871–1938) was one of the first African-American professors at New York University.

Johnson was head of the National Association for the Advancement of Colored People from 1920 to 1930. During this period, he worked to help African-American writers get published. Through his own writings, he challenged racial stereotypes, fought segregation, and argued for anti-lynching laws.

PROMOTING BLACK HISTORY

The accomplishments of historian and journalist Carter Woodson (1875–1950) are remarkable, given his background. He was the son of former slaves, but had few chances to attend school when growing up. He was mostly self-taught until he was 20 years old. Then he had the chance to attend a black high school in West Virginia. After graduating, he taught school for a few years, then went to college. He earned a bachelor's degree from Berea College in Kentucky. Then, he attended the University of Chicago and earned a master's degree. Finally, in 1912, he became just the second African American to earn a Ph.D from Harvard University.

Woodson believed that blacks needed to be aware of their important contributions to American history. In 1915 he and the Reverend Jesse Moreland, a minister and community leader, founded the Association for the Study of Negro Life and History. The organization's purpose was to educate people about African-American life, history, and culture. In 1916, the organization began publishing a scholarly journal, which Woodson edited until he died.

"If We Must Die"

One of Claude McKay's best-known poems is titled "If We Must Die." It was written about race riots in 1919. At the time, whites were attacking black neighborhoods in a number of cities. McKay's message was that it was better to die fighting than to surrender and be killed, even when the odds are against a person. The last two lines are: "Like men we'll face the murderous, cowardly pack, / Pressed to the wall, dying, but fighting back!"

During World War II, British prime minister Winston Churchill quoted from the poem. He wanted to inspire his countrymen to fight against Nazi Germany.

In addition to writing many articles for the *Journal of Negro History*, Woodson also wrote important history books. One was about the education of African Americans before the Civil War. Another book was about black churches. A third was about black professionals, such as lawyers and doctors. He wrote textbooks that were widely used. One of them was *The Negro in Our History* (1922). Woodson also collected the

Carter Woodson started Negro History Week in February 1926 to celebrate the birthdays of Abraham Lincoln and Frederick Douglass. Today, we recognize February as Black History Month.

writings of notable African Americans, including Frederick Douglass and Booker T. Washington. Because of his accomplishments, Woodson is called the Father of Black History.

AFRICAN-AMERICAN NOVELISTS

Most writers of the Harlem Renaissance celebrated their color. Jean Toomer (1894–1967) was different. He didn't want to be labeled a "black" writer. Toomer had light skin, and at times he "passed" as white. At other times he lived as a black man. After a while, Toomer only wanted to be labeled American. His 1923 book *Cane* explores this theme. *Cane* is a combination of poetry, short stories, and drama. It was considered a masterpiece, and influenced many modern African-American writers.

By all accounts, Zora Neale Hurston lit up a room. Nicknamed "Queen of the Renaissance," she wrote four novels and more than 50 short stories, plays, and essays. She was at the center of the Harlem Renaissance, and was a major African-American literary figure during the 1930s. However, by the early 1950s Hurston's popularity had faded. She was living in poverty, largely forgotten, at the time of her death in 1960.

Arnaud "Arna" Bontemps (1902–1973) was a notable novelist and poet. His best-known works included the novels *God Sends Sunday* (1931) and *Black Thunder* (1936). His children's book about African-American history, *Story of the Negro*, won the Newbery Medal in 1949.

Another influential novelist of the Harlem Renaissance was Zora Neale Hurston (1891–1960). Hurston combined her writing skills with other talents. She collected folklore. A folklorist studies the beliefs, legends, and customs of a group. She was also an anthropologist, someone who studies human beings and their relationships. One of Hurston's best-known works was *Mules and Men* (1935), a collection of African-American folklore. Her novel *Their Eyes Were Watching God* was published in 1937. It is the story of a young woman figuring out who she is.

* * *

The beginning of the end of the Harlem Renaissance came with the beginning of the Great Depression in 1929. Providing food and shelter became more important than following the latest literary trends. It wasn't until decades later that scholars began to study the Harlem Renaissance and to realize its importance in shaping African-American writing.

Ralph Ellison was an American novelist and literary critic. Best known for his National Book Award-winning novel *Invisible Man* (1952), Ellison's other major works include the essay collections *Shadow and Act* (1964) and *Going to the Territory* (1986).

5

WWII AND BEYOND:
FUELING THE CIVIL RIGHTS MOVEMENT

I n the 1940s and beyond, African-American literature entered an excit-
ing and changing period. One of the most important works of fiction
written at this time was Richard Wright's novel *Native Son*. Published
in 1940, *Native Son* was the first novel by an African American to hit the
bestseller list.

Native Son is violent. It made readers uncomfortable. The main character, a young black man named Bigger Thomas, lives with his family in a
tiny, rat-infested apartment in Chicago. He lives with a sense of hopeless-
ness, believing he'll never escape from his awful situation. Thomas is a
troublemaker, but he gets a job with the Dalton family. They are white.
They like to talk about their support for blacks. Yet it turns out they own
the unlivable apartment building that Bigger and his family live in.

Although it's not his fault, Bigger ends up in an awkward situation with
Mary Dalton, the daughter. Acting out of fear, he accidentally kills her.
Bigger's fear, and the expectations that American society has of black men,
then sets him on a course of further violence.

ASKING DIFFICULT QUESTIONS
Wright (1908–1960) challenged readers to think about tough questions:

Most of Richard Wright's works dealt with the issue of race and American society. He would eventually leave the United States altogether, spending the last 14 years of his life in France.

Does the injustice of American society deserve some blame for Bigger's crime? How much does a person's living environment control their actions? What role does Bigger's lack of choices play?

Wright wanted to open people's eyes to the world of African Americans. He realistically showed the extreme poverty in which many blacks lived. He showed how common oppression and racism were. He hoped his writing would influence changes in society.

Richard Wright became famous worldwide. He wrote many powerful short stories and essays, as well as novels. His memoir *Black Boy* (1945) is a vivid look at his bleak childhood in the South. It was another bestseller. In 1946, Wright left the United States forever. He moved to Paris, where he continued to write until his death.

ANOTHER WAY TO LOOK AT RACE

Richard Wright inspired many other African-American writers. One of them was James Baldwin (1924–1987). In the mid-1940s, Wright helped Baldwin get his start as a writer. However, their friendship ended in 1949, when Baldwin wrote an essay that criticized *Native Son*.

Baldwin had a beautiful and powerful way with words. His first novel was *Go Tell It on the Mountain* (1953). The book was based on his upbringing in Harlem. Like Baldwin's stepfather, the stepfather in the book is a preacher. It is considered a classic.

Baldwin and Wright had different ideas about racial issues. Wright wrote about the effect racism had on African-Americans. Baldwin argued that racism also had a negative impact on white Americans. He believed

that everyone suffers in a racist society.

Ideas about race were changing in the United States during this period. In 1948, President Harry Truman ordered the integration of the armed forces. In 1954, the U.S. Supreme Court ended half a century of "separate but equal" policies with a ruling in *Brown v. Board of Education*. The court said that public schools should no longer be segregated. These decisions helped end segregation in other areas as well. In 1955, Rosa Parks refused to give up her seat in the "white" section of a Montgomery, Alabama, bus. Eventually, the Supreme Court ruled that public transportation could not be segregated, either. African-Americans saw these important changes as victories in the movement to gain rights equal to white Americans.

James Baldwin lectured and wrote in

Like Richard Wright, James Baldwin left the United States hoping to find greater freedom in France. His 1953 novel *Go Tell It on the Mountain* is about racism and the role of the Christian church in black life.

support of the Civil Rights Movement. He also continued to write powerful essays examining what it was like to be a black man in the United States. In his 1963 book *The Fire Next Time*, Baldwin predicted that if whites and blacks couldn't work out their racial issues, violence would follow. However, he also wrote of his hope for the future: "We may be able, handful that we are, to end the racial nightmare, and achieve our country, and change the history of the world."

INVISIBLE MAN

Another African-American writer whom Richard Wright inspired was Ralph Ellison (1914–1994). Ellison had been a music student at Tuskegee, but turned to writing after moving to Harlem in the mid-1930s. There he met Langston Hughes, who introduced him to Richard Wright. Wright

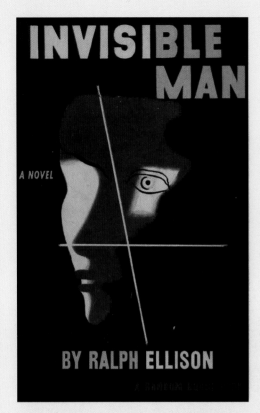

Invisible Man, Ralph Ellison's master-piece, addresses many of the social issues that blacks faced in the 1950s.

befriended Ellison, and helped him get a job as a writer in 1938. Ellison worked for the Federal Writers' Project. This was a program that was part of Franklin Roosevelt's New Deal. Writers were hired to interview people, such as former slaves, about their life histories. They also wrote histories of local communities and guide-books. Ellison learned a lot about African-American history and folklore while work-ing with the project. In his spare time, he published many articles and short stories.

In 1952, Ellison's novel *Invisible Man* was published. The main character of *Invisible Man* is the opposite of Bigger Thomas. He's educated and thoughtful. He's faced some challenges, but he arrives in Harlem optimistic about his future. Things go downhill quickly, however. He ends up living in an underground hole. He believes he is invisible. It's not that people don't see him. He's invisible because peo-ple see a black man and then they think they know all about him.

The writing style reflected Ellison's love of jazz music. The narrator's tone varies throughout the book, from sad to loud to playful to fast, and others. Certain things are repeated like a refrain.

Invisible Man was a bestseller for months. It won the National Book Award in 1953. Ellison was the first African American to earn the award. It has been called one of the most important works of fiction from the twentieth century.

Ellison continued writing and teaching for the rest of his life. He never finished another novel, however. After his death, an editor went through

thousands of fiction pages that Ellison had been working on for over 40 years. He used the pages to create a new book, called *Juneteenth*. The title refers to June 19, 1865—a date commemorated as the end of slavery in the South.

OUTSTANDING FEMALE WRITERS

Two African-American women stand out as major writers during the 1950s and 1960s. One was a poet, Gwendolyn Brooks (1917–2000). The other was a playwright, Lorraine Hansberry (1930–1965).

The poetry of Gwendolyn Brooks was about the day-to-day lives of African Americans, particularly those living in cities. She wrote about discrimination against blacks. She also wrote about lighter-skinned blacks who discriminated against darker-skinned people. She wrote poetry calling for racial harmony.

Brooks wrote in many styles. Sometimes her poems were very structured. Other poems were written in free verse. Sometimes her vocabulary was difficult. Other times she used the street language of African Americans.

Gwendolyn Brooks's first poems appeared in the *Chicago Defender* when she was a teenager in the 1930s. Her first book of

One of Gwendolyn Brooks's best known poems is "We Real Cool," written in 1959. This poster version of the poem, produced in the mid-1960s, was meant to be posted publicly.

poetry, *A Street in Bronzeville*, was published in 1945. In 1950, her poetry collection *Annie Allen* won the Pulitzer Prize. Brooks was the first African American to earn this prestigious award for writing. She received many other awards and honors during long career as a writer.

Unlike Brooks, Lorraine Hansberry had a short writing career. She died of cancer at age 34. However, her play *A Raisin in the Sun* is considered an

Journalist Marvel Jackson Cooke

Marvel Jackson Cooke (1903–2000) was the first African-American woman to work for a mainstream white-owned newspaper. After graduating from college, she arrived in Harlem in 1926. She was soon hired by W.E.B. Du Bois to write a column for the NAACP's magazine, *The Crisis*. This job led to other journalism jobs.

In 1928, Cooke became the first woman reporter hired at the *New York Amsterdam News*, a black paper. She helped organize other workers there into a labor union. They protested against the paper's unfair wages. She was arrested twice. Eventually, the newspaper was sold to another company. The new owners gave the employees raises. The experience made history in several ways. It was the first time black workers had protested against a black employer, and it was the first time African-Americans workers had won a labor dispute.

In 1950, she wrote her most famous articles. She wrote about black women standing on street corners, waiting to be hired by wealthy white women to work as maids for the day. To research the articles, she stood with the women and hired herself out. The first day, she quit when her employer claimed she had missed two panes in the window she was washing. Another day, she was paid $3.40 for washing, ironing, and scrubbing floors all day long.

Cooke wrote the series, called "The Bronx Slave Market" when she was the only woman, and the only African American, on the staff of the *New York Daily Compass*. The paper was owned by whites.

important work of African-American literature. It was the first play written by an African-American woman to become a Broadway hit. *A Raisin in the Sun* won many awards, including best play of 1959.

In the play, an African-American family, the Youngers, comes into some money. Five of them have been crowded into a small apartment. They have different ideas about how to use the money, based on their dreams for the future. They decide to buy a house in a better neighborhood, thinking that they'll have a chance at better lives. Then the adult son, Walter, makes a bad decision and loses some of the money. It was supposed to have paid for his sister's education. Soon it becomes clear they Youngers are not wanted in the all-white neighborhood where they've chosen to live. Walter must decide. Should he sell the house to a white man? He could sell for more than the family paid for it. He would recover the money that he lost. Or, Walter can stand up for his family's rights and stay. This would give his young son Travis a chance to receive the education that Walter never had.

Lorraine Hansberry

Hansberry made her play about working-class people. This was unusual. James Baldwin said, "I had never in my life seen so many black people in the theater. And the reason was that never before, in the entire history of the American theater, had so much of the truth of black people's lives been seen on the stage."

A Raisin in the Sun made Hansberry famous. She wrote many other things before she died. At her funeral, a letter by Dr. Martin Luther King Jr. was read. King wrote, "Her creative ability and her profound grasp of the deep social issues confronting the world today will remain an inspiration to generations yet unborn."

= Did You Know? =

The title *A Raisin in the Sun* came from a Langston Hughes poem. In the poem, Hughes asked what happened to dreams that are put off: Do they dry up, like a raisin in the sun? Or do they explode?

Acclaimed poet, writer, and activist Maya Angelou (b. 1928) has won dozens of awards for her writing. The first of her her six autobiographical works, *I Know Why the Caged Bird Sings* (1969), focuses on the many challenges she faced during her first 17 years of life. The book made her famous, and remains popular among young students.

6

CONTEMPORARY AFRICAN-AMERICAN WRITERS

During the 1960s, the civil rights movement was in full swing. African Americans expressed pride in their history, culture, and accomplishments. Some took this pride a step further. They felt that African Americans should build their own political and economic systems, separate from those of whites. Around 1966, the term "black power" was coined. To many African Americans, black power meant being willing to fight for their rights.

Many notable African-American writers were inspired by the changing times. As a result, the period from 1965 to 1976 is called the "Black Arts Movement." The Black Arts Movement is sometimes called the Second Renaissance. There were differences, though. The original Harlem Renaissance was centered in New York. The Black Arts Movement happened in many places throughout the country. Also, black artists of the 1960s were angrier and more confrontational than writers of the Harlem Renaissance had been.

KEY BLACK ARTS FIGURES

One founder of the Black Arts Movement was Amiri Baraka (1934-   ). He was a well-known poet and writer in the early 1960s. As the decade progressed, his writing became bolder. His 1969 poem "Black Art" called for violence to establish a black society. Baraka's work has offended many people during his career. He was once quoted as saying, "We must eliminate the white man before we can draw a free breath on this planet." Others admire him for his boldness in stating what he believes and his uncompromising attitude.

Haki Madhubuti (1942-) first became known as a poet. In 1967, he started Third World Press. His company has published many other African American writers. He has also spent many years as a college professor. He has given hundreds of workshops, readings, and school visits. His books have sold more than 3 million copies.

The work of Adrienne Kennedy (1931-) is bold and unusual. Kennedy's plays started getting produced during the 1960s. They usually contain strange plot twists, odd characters, and lots of symbolism. Many of Kennedy's plays are about race in American society. Her plots are not always easy to understand. Her best-known plays include *Funnyhouse of a Negro* (1964), *A Rat's Mass* (1967), and *June and Jean in Concert* (1995). Kennedy has received many awards and honors throughout the years.

Mari Evans (1923-) is a celebrated poet of the Black Arts Movement. During the 1970s she became known for her poetry. She experimented

The web site of Third World Press. Founded by Haki R. Madhubuti in 1967, today it is the largest independent press in the United States owned by an African American.

with capitalization and unusual line lengths. Poems like "I am a Black Woman" (1970) express the joy of African-American life:

I am a black woman
tall as a cypress
strong
beyond all definition still
defying place
and time
and circumstance
assailed
impervious
indestructible
Look
on me and be
renewed

In addition to poetry, Evans has been a successful playwright, children's author, television director, and editor. She has taught at colleges and universities and has received numerous honors.

Another innovative writer of the Black Arts Movement was Ntozake Shange (1948-   ). In 1975 she invented a type of play that she called a choreopoem. This means a blend of poetry, dance, and music. In *For Colored Girls Who Have Considered Suicide When the Rainbow is Enuf*, seven female characters use 20 poems to present difficulties and challenges faced by African-American women. The play emphasizes the power of women's relationships. The play was made into a

movie, *For Colored Girls*, in 2010. Issues related to women and race are common in Shange's other work, which includes novels, children's books, and essays.

THE SAGA OF ROOTS

In 1976, Alex Haley (1921–1992) wrote a book called *Roots: The Saga of an American Family*. It was the story of a man named Kunta Kinte, who was born in Africa in 1750. The book told the story of Kunta Kinte's capture by slave traders and voyage to America on a slave ship. The book describes Kinte's repeated efforts to escape slavery. *Roots* also tells the story of Kinte's daughter, Kizzy, and her descendants. One of them is said to be Haley himself.

This statue of Alex Haley is located near the harbor in Annapolis, Maryland, where the African slave Kunta Kinte was brought to America in 1767.

Roots was incredibly successful. The book spent nearly a year on the best-seller list. It sold 1.5 million copies its first year. It was made into a hit television miniseries in 1977. The TV show was viewed by millions of people, and won many awards. Haley also received a special Pulitzer Prize for his work that year.

Although Haley originally said *Roots* was a true story about his ancestors, other researchers found errors in the tale. Haley apparently made up some parts of the story. It also turned out that Haley may have copied some material from other sources. Yet the popularity of *Roots* was astonishingly huge, both with black and white readers. Despite its faults, *Roots* is still an important work of literature.

MODERN-DAY PRIZE WINNERS

In 1993, Toni Morrison (1931-   ) became the first African American to win the Nobel Prize in Literature. Morrison is known for her authentic dialogue and poetic language. Her first novel, *The Bluest Eye* (1970), tells the story of an abused girl. The girl fantasizes that her life would be fine if she just had blue eyes, light hair, and skin. In the end, she loses her mind. She lives in a fantasy world where she does indeed have the bluest eye of all.

Morrison's best-known book is *Beloved* (1987), her fifth novel. She won the Pulitzer Prize for Fiction for this book. The story centers around a woman, Sethe. She kills her child rather than see her become a slave. Years later, Sethe is haunted by the child's ghost. Finally the ghost disappears. Or so it seems, until one day a young woman arrives. She seems to be the mur-

Charlayne Hunter-Gault

As a teenager in the late 1950s, Charlayne Hunter-Gault made national news. Despite an excellent high school record, she was turned down when she applied to the University of Georgia in 1959. No African American had ever been admitted to the school. She sued the school and won. She began classes in 1961.

Even before she became part of a news story, Hunter-Gault knew she wanted to be a journalist. Ignoring harassment, she worked toward her goal in college, graduating in 1963. She launched her career as a television reporter in Washington, D.C. Then she went to work at the *New York Times* in 1968. In 1978, she began working as a correspondent for National Public Radio's news programs. She later worked as a reporter for CNN.

Hunter-Gault is known for reporting on the human stories that are part of larger political stories. She has won many awards, including the 1986 Journalist of the Year Award from the National Association of Black Journalists.

In 2012, Toni Morrison received the Presidential Medal of Freedom, the most prestigious award the U.S. government can award to a civilian.

dered daughter. In recent years, Morrison's novels include *Jazz* (1992), *Paradise* (1997), *Love* (2003), *A Mercy* (2008), and *Home* (2012).

Alice Walker (1944-   ) writes novels, poetry, essays, and more. Her best-known work is *The Color Purple* (1982). This novel tells the story of an abused, poor black woman. Because of some women in her life, the story comes to an uplifting end. *The Color Purple* won the Pulitzer Prize for Literature and the National Book Award for fiction. Walker became the first African-American woman to win both of these awards.

Another National Book Award winner is Charles R. Johnson (1948-   ). His first novel, *Faith and the Good Thing* (1974) received good reviews. Some compared it to Ralph Ellison's *Invisible Man*. Johnson's third novel, *Middle Passage*, is about a voyage by a slave ship. It won the National Book Award in 1990.

As a teenager, Edward P. Jones (1950-   ) discovered the works of Richard Wright and other black writers. He later told *Publishers Weekly* he felt "as if they were talking to me . . . [the] books had people in them that I knew in my own life." Jones's first book, a collection of short stories called *Lost in the City*, was nominated for a National Book Award in 1992. He spent years thinking about his next book. *The Known World* won him another National Book Award nomination and the Pulitzer Prize for Fiction in 2004. The novel was inspired by a little-known fact—some free black Americans owned slaves. The book is set in the 1850s. Jones has explained,

"I want to write about the things which helped us to survive: the love, grace, intelligence and strength for us as a people."

August Wilson (1945–2005) is another modern Pulitzer Prize winner. He wrote ten plays about African-American life in the 20th century. Each play is set at a different time. All but one is set in Pittsburgh, where Wilson was born.

> = Did You Know? =
>
> By the 1960s, Zora Neale Hurston's writing had nearly been forgotten. A 1975 article by Alice Walker helped renew interest in Hurston's work.

Wilson's plays deal with people who are struggling. He wrote about cab-drivers, maids, garbagemen, and criminals. The *New York Times* described his work as dealing with "universal truths about the struggle for dignity, love, security and happiness in the face of often overwhelming obstacles." The paper described his dialogue as a having "the complexity of jazz" and the "emotional power of the blues." He has been called "a giant figure in American theater." His plays *Fences* (1987) and *The Piano Lesson* (1990) each won the Pulitzer Prize for Drama.

The playwright August Wilson credited poet Amiri Baraka as an influence on his writing. In addition to his two Pulitzer Prize-winning plays, Wilson's best-known works include *Ma Rainey's Black Bottom* (1982), *Joe Turner's Come and Gone* (1984), and his final play, *Radio Golf* (2005).

CHAPTER NOTES

p. 10:   "not wish to be free . . ." Jupiter Hammon, "An Address to the Negroes of the State of New York" (1787). Reprinted in Leslie M. Harris, *In the Shadow of Slavery: African Americans in New York City, 1626-1863* (Chicago: University of Chicago Press, 2003), p. 67

p. 12:   "broken in body, soul, and spirit," Frederick Douglass, *Narrative of the Life of Frederick Douglass, An American Slave.* (1845). http://sunsite.berkeley.edu/Literature/Douglass.

p. 14:   "I discovered that the power . . ." Frederick Douglass, quoted in Amy Anderson, "The Path to Freedom: How the Education of Frederick Douglass Helped Change the Nation" *Success* (August 2009). http://www.success.com/articles/764-profiles-in-greatness-frederick-douglass.

p. 14:   "America, it is to thee . . ." James Monroe Whitfield, "America" (1853). http://www.historyisaweapon.com/defcon1/whitamer.html.

p. 21:   "I ask no monument . . ." Frances E. W. Harper, "Bury Me in a Free Land" (1856). http://www.theotherpages.org/poems/2001/harper0105.html.

p. 23:   "jingle in a broken tongue," Paul Laurence Dunbar, "The Poet" (1903). http://www.gutenberg.org/cache/epub/18338/pg18338.txt.

p. 26:   "There is, therefore, only one thing . . ." Ida Wells, quoted in H.W. Brands, *American Colossus: The Triumph of Capitalism, 1865-1900* (New York: Doubleday, 2010), p. 398.

p. 31:   "We didn't exist . . ." Vernon Jarrett, quoted in *The Black Press: Soldiers Without Swords.* http://www.pbs.org/blackpress/film/index.html.

p. 34:   "intend to express our individual . . ." Langston Hughes, "The Negro Artist and the Racial Mountain" (1926). http://www.poetryfoundation.org/learning/poetics-essay.html?id=237858&page=2.

p. 34:   "I, Too, Sing America . . ." Langston Hughes, "I, Too" (1925). http://www.poetryfoundation.org/archive/poem.html?id=177020.

p. 37:   "Like men we'll face . . ." Claude McKay, "If We Must Die" (1919). http://www.poetryfoundation.org/archive/poem.html?id=173960.

p. 38:   "jump at de sun," Zora Neale Hurston,
           http://www.zoranealehurston.com/biography.html.

p. 43:   "We may be able . . ." James Baldwin, quoted in Sheldon Binn, "The
           Fire Next Time" (*The New York Times*, January 31, 1963)

p. 47:   "I had never in my life seen . . ." James Baldwin, quoted in Steven C.
           Tracy, *Writers of the Black Chicago Renaissance* (Champaign:
           University of Illinois Press, 2011), p. 199.

p. 47:   "Her creative ability . . ." Martin Luther King, Jr., quoted in *Gale
           Contemporary Black Biography*. http://www.answers.com/topic/lor-
           raine-hansberry.

p. 50:   "We must eliminate the white . . ." Amiri Baraka, quoted by Petri
           Liukkonen. http://www.kirjasto.sci.fi/baraka.htm.

p. 51:   "I am a black woman . . ." Mari Evans, "I am a Black Woman" (1970).
           http://www.math.buffalo.edu/~sww/poetry/evans_mari.html#I%20am%
           20a%20Black%20Woman.

p. 54:   "as if they were talking . . ." Edward P. Jones, quoted in Robert
           Fleming, "Just Stating the Case is 'More Than Enough'" *Publishers
           Weekly* 250, no. 32 (August 8, 2003), p. 254.

p. 55:   "I want to write about . . ." Fleming, "Just Stating the Case is 'More
           Than Enough.'"

p. 55:   "universal truths about . . . ." Charles Isherwood, "August Wilson,
           Theater's Poet of Black America, Is Dead at 60," *The New York Times*
           (October 3, 2005), p. T1.

p. 55:   "the complexity of jazz," Ibid.

p. 55:   "a giant figure in American theater" Ibid.

CHRONOLOGY

1746: Lucy Terry writes "Bars Fight," the first known poem by an African American; it is transmitted orally and not published until 1855.

1760: Briton Hammon's *Narrative* is published in Boston.

1761: Jupiter Hammon becomes the first African American to have poetry published.

1827: *Freedom's Journal*, the first African American newspaper, is founded in New York on March 16.

1845: *Narrative of the Life of Frederick Douglass* is published.

1859: Frances E.W. Harper publishes *Our Nig*, the first novel by an African American.

1901: Booker T. Washington's autobiography *Up From Slavery* stresses the need for blacks to become educated in order to succeed in America.

1903: W.E.B. Du Bois's book *The Souls of Black Folk* is published.

1925: Alain Locke's anthology *The New Negro: An Interpretation*, an important literary work of the Harlem Renaissance, is published.

1926: Carter Woodson starts Negro History Week to commemorate the birthdays of Frederick Douglass and Abraham Lincoln, in February.

1950: Gwendolyn Brooks is the first black poet to win the Pulitzer Prize.

1953: Ralph Ellison becomes the first African American to win the National Book Award (for *Invisible Man*).

1976: Alex Haley's *Roots: The Saga of an American Family* becomes a best-seller and is turned into a highly successful television miniseries.

1982: Alice Walker's novel *The Color Purple* wins both the Pulitzer Prize and the American Book Award.

1993: Toni Morrison becomes the first African American to win the Nobel Prize in Literature; Rita Dove is the first black female to serve as poet laureate of the United States.

2004: Edward P. Jones wins the Pulitzer Prize for *The Known World*.

2012: Toni Morrison receives the Presidential Medal of Freedom, the highest civilian award given by the U.S. government.

GLOSSARY

abolition—the movement to end slavery in the United States.

activism—taking direct, possibly confrontational, action to achieve a goal.

almanac—a book that contains a calendar, weather forecasts, and other information.

autobiography—the story of a person's life.

classic—recognized as being of the highest quality in its field, such as a classic book.

dialect—a variety of speech used by a certain group, such as in a certain region or of the same heritage.

folklore—the study of the beliefs, legends, and customs of a group of people.

free verse—verse without a rhyme or consistent pattern.

genre—category of writing, such as poetry, nonfiction, children's, and so on.

integration—bringing together different groups into one equal community.

narrative—a story or telling of events; may be fact or fiction.

playwright—a person who writes plays.

prose—ordinary writing; not poetry.

publisher—the person or company responsible for getting a book, magazine, newspaper, or other piece of writing printed.

segregate—separated or set apart from others

yellow journalism—journalism that exaggerates or distorts the news in order to attract readers.

FURTHER READING

Hill, Laban Carrick. *Harlem Stomp! A Cultural History of the Harlem Renaissance*. New York: Little, Brown Books for Young Readers, 2009.

Magill, Frank N., ed. *Masterpieces of African American Literature*. New York: HarperCollins Publishers, 1993.

Robson, David. *The Black Arts Movement*. San Diego: Lucent, 2008.

Russell, Sandi. *Render Me My Song: African American Women Writers From Slavery to the Present*. New York: St. Martin's Press, 1990.

Streitmatter, Rodger. *Raising Her Voice: African American Journalist Who Changed History*. Lexington: the University Press of Kentucky, 1994.

INTERNET RESOURCES

http://www.pbs.org/blackpress/index.html

The official web site of the PBS documentary *The Black Press: Soldiers Without Swords* provides information on black newspapers, biographies of African-American journalists, and a timeline.

http://www.loc.gov/rr/program/bib/btwashington/index.html

This is a Library of Congress compilation of information and resources on Booker T. Washington, including links to his writings.

http://www.poetryfoundation.org

The Poetry Foundation web site provides biographical information and poetry of many poets. It also contains audio clips of poetry readings, such as Langston Hughes reading his poem, "I've Known Rivers."

http://www.pbs.org/wgbh/aia/home.html

The PBS web site for *Africans in America* provides background information on the history of African Americans from 1450 to 1865.

http://www.csustan.edu/english/reuben/pal/chap9/9intro.html

This web site provides information on the Harlem Renaissance, including a chronology, biographies and lists of works of numerous Harlem Renaissance writers.

http://memory.loc.gov/ammem/doughtml/doughome.html

The Library of Congress has papers of Frederick Douglass online, as well as a timeline.

http://www.libraries.wright.edu/special/dunbar/

The Paul Laurence Dunbar Digital Collection from Wright State University has the text of many of Dunbar's poems.

INDEX

Numbers in **bold italics** refer to captions.

CONTRIBUTORS

MARY HERTZ SCARBROUGH is the author of more than a dozen nonfiction books for children. She loves to research and write about history. She lives in South Dakota with her family.

Senior Consulting Editor **DR. MARC LAMONT HILL** is one of the leading hip-hop generation intellectuals in the country. Dr. Hill has lectured widely and provides regular commentary for media outlets like NPR, the *Washington Post*, *Essence Magazine*, the *New York Times*, CNN, MSNBC, and *The O'Reilly Factor*. He is the host of the nationally syndicated television show *Our World With Black Enterprise*. Dr. Hill is a columnist and editor-at-large for the *Philadelphia Daily News*. His books include the award-winning *Beats, Rhymes, and Classroom Life: Hip-Hop Pedagogy and the Politics of Identity* (2009).

Since 2009 Dr. Hill has been on the faculty of Columbia University as Associate Professor of Education at Teachers College. He holds an affiliated faculty appointment in African American Studies at the Institute for Research in African American Studies at Columbia University.

Since his days as a youth in Philadelphia, Dr. Hill has been a social justice activist and organizer. He is a founding board member of My5th, a non-profit organization devoted to educating youth about their legal rights and responsibilities. He is also a board member and organizer of the Philadelphia Student Union. Dr. Hill also works closely with the ACLU Drug Reform Project, focusing on drug informant policy. In addition to his political work, Dr. Hill continues to work directly with African American and Latino youth.

In 2005, *Ebony* named Dr. Hill one of America's 100 most influential Black leaders. The magazine had previously named him one of America's top 30 Black leaders under 30 years old.